YEAR 2
MATHEMATICS
National Curriculum Tests

ꕙSCHOLASTIC

Published in the UK by Scholastic Education, 2020

Book End, Range Road, Witney, Oxfordshire, OX29 0YD

A division of Scholastic Limited

London - New York - Toronto - Sydney - Auckland

Mexico City - New Delhi - Hong Kong

SCHOLASTIC and associated logos are trademarks and/or registered trademarks of Scholastic Inc.

www.scholastic.co.uk

© 2017, 2020 Scholastic Limited

1 2 3 4 5 6 7 8 9   0 1 2 3 4 5 6 7 8 9

A British Library Cataloguing-in-Publication Data
A catalogue record for this book is available from the British Library.

ISBN 978-1407-18360-2

Printed and bound by Replika Press, India

Author
Caroline Clissold

Editorial team
Rachel Morgan, Jenny Wilcox, Kim Vernon and Julia Roberts

Illustrations
Tom Heard

Design
Nicolle Thomas and Oxford Designers and Illustrators

Acknowledgements

Extracts from Department for Education website © Crown Copyright. Reproduced under the terms of the Open Government Licence (OGL). www.nationalarchives.gov.uk/doc/open-government-licence/version/2

Every effort has been made to trace copyright holders for the works reproduced in this book, and the publishers apologise or any inadvertent omissions.

Contents for Mathematics: Booster Tests Year 2

About this book

This book is part of the Scholastic Booster Programme. The series provides you with practice papers and a workbook of support activities to help children with the Key Stage 1 Mathematics National Test. There is also a teacher's guide provided in the classroom pack. It provides valuable practice of the content expected of Year 2 children (aged 6–7 years).

In the book you will find two mathematics tests. The style and layout of each test closely matches that used in the National Curriculum Tests, so children will become familiar with the format and know what to expect.

At the end of each test is a marks table where you can record the children's results. This table also references workbook pages that relate to the topic of each question. If your child needs more support in any area, then direct them to the workbook for further practice. The workbook can also be used for general practice of the skills and knowledge the children will need for the tests.

About the tests

Each mathematics test has two papers:

- Paper 1: arithmetic – these are context-free calculations. The children have approximately 20 minutes to answer the questions. 25 marks are available. A practice question is provided at the start of the paper.

- Paper 2: reasoning – these are mathematical reasoning problems both in context and out of context. The children have approximately 35 minutes to answer the questions. 35 marks are available. A practice question is provided at the start of the paper and then followed by five aural questions.

The papers should be taken in order and children may have a break between papers. Neither paper should be strictly timed. You should ensure that every child has enough time to demonstrate what he or she understands, knows and can do, without prolonging the test inappropriately. Use your judgement to decide when, or if, children need breaks during the assessment, and whether to stop the text early if appropriate.

Do the practice question for each test together and ensure the children write their answer in the correct place.

All of the tests broadly increase in difficulty as they progress, and it is not expected that all children will be able to answer all of the questions. All questions can be read aloud so that reading ability does not affect a child's ability to demonstrate their mathematical skills.

The marks available for each question are shown next to each question and are also shown next to each answer in the mark scheme.

Aural questions

 There are five aural questions in paper 2. They are shown by this symbol. These questions should be read aloud following the script on page 88 of this book.

Using the practice papers

Using practice tests will help to build children's confidence as well as their ability to work to a time limit. The children will need to be familiar with specific test-focused skills, such as reading carefully, leaving questions until the end if they seem too difficult, working at a suitable pace and checking through their work.

It is recommended that children take one of the tests at the beginning of the booster programme to assess their knowledge and understanding. The marks table at end of each reasoning test has a 'Strand' and a 'Sub-strand' column, which will help you to identify areas in which the children need more practice and direct you to relevant pages in the workbook.

A period of revision should then follow, focusing on weaker areas using the workbook. The children can then take another test at the end of the programme to ensure understanding has been consolidated.

Advice for parents and carers

The timings below are given as suggestions, school programmes may be set over a longer timescale. The key is to provide children with lots of support and practice in the run up to the test.

Six weeks before the test:

- Read through Test A Papers 1–2 so that you know what the child will be doing. You could even try Test A yourself so you know how difficult it is.

- Let the child take Test A Papers 1–2 under examination conditions. Do not help them.

- Go through the answers and mark the test together. Talk about which parts of the test the child found difficult.

- Make a list of areas for further revision and encourage children to practise these areas for one hour a week using the workbook and the test paper.

Four weeks before the test:

- Look at Test A Papers 1–2 again with the child. Use the workbook to provide extra practice in areas the child struggled with.

- Review any workbook activities together. Go through the answers. Talk about the parts of the test the child found difficult. Encourage them to continuing practising.

Two weeks before the test:

- Look at the Test A papers again with the child. Use the workbook to provide extra support in the areas the child found most difficult.

- Let your child take Test B Papers 1–2 under examination conditions. Do not help them.

- Go through the answers and mark the test together. Talk about which parts of the test the child found difficult. If they are the same parts as before, offer or seek specific support for the child in this area.

- In the remaining two weeks, go through each of the tests again together, concentrating on the areas the child has found difficult.

General preparation for the practice tests:

- Make sure that you allow the child to take the practice test in a quiet environment where they are not likely to be interrupted or distracted.

- Make sure the child has a flat surface to work on with plenty of space to spread out, and good light.

- Emphasise the importance of reading and re-reading a question and to underline or circle any important information.

- If you are unsure of anything yourself, then make an appointment to see your child's teacher who will be able to help and advise further.

Advice for children

What to do before the test

- Revise and practise regularly.
- Spend some time each week practising.
- Focus on the areas you are less sure of to get better.
- Get a good night's sleep and eat a healthy breakfast.
- Be on time for school.
- Make sure you have all the things you need.

During the test:

- Read the questions carefully. Then read them again.
- If a questions asks you to 'Show your method' then there will be marks if you get the method correct even if your answer is wrong.
- If you're struggling with a question, move on and return to it at the end.
- Write as clearly as you can.
- Use every minute of the test time. If you've finished, check your answers!

Test coverage

The test content is divided into strands and sub-strands. These are listed, for each question, in a table on the back cover of every test to allow tracking of difficulties. In a small number of cases, where practical equipment such as containers would be required, these aspects are not tested.

Strand	Sub-strand
Number and place value	counting (in multiples)
	read, write, order and compare numbers
	identify, represent and rounding
	number problems
Addition, subtraction, multiplication and division (calculations)	add/subtract mentally
	add/subtract using written methods
	use inverses and check
	add/subtract to solve problems
	multiply/divide mentally
	multiply/divide using written methods
	solve problems based on all four operations and knowledge of the commutative facts
	order operations
Fractions	recognise, find, write, name and count fractions
	equivalent fractions
Measurement	compare, describe and order measures
	measure and read scales
	money
	telling time, ordering time and units of time
	solve mathematical problems involving measures
Geometry – properties of shape	recognise and name common shapes
	describe properties and classify shapes
	draw and make shapes and relate 2D and 3D shapes
Geometry – position and direction	patterns
	describe position, direction and movement
Statistics	interpret and represent data
	solve problems involving data

Mathematics

Test A: Paper 1

Instructions Test A: Paper 1

- You have around **20 minutes** to complete this test paper.
- You may **not use** a calculator for any questions in this test paper.
- Work as quickly and carefully as you can.
- Try to answer all the questions. If you cannot do one of the questions, **go on to the next one**. You can come back to it later, if you have time.
- If you finish before the end, **go back and check your work**.
- Ask your teacher if you are not sure what to do.

Follow the instructions for each question carefully.

If you need to do working out, you can use any space on the page – do not use rough paper.

Practice question

Marks

$10 = 3 +$ ☐

Test A: Paper I

I.

$$7 + 3 = \boxed{}$$

Marks

1

2.

$$10 = 8 + \boxed{}$$

1

Marks

3. $69 + 1 = \boxed{}$

1

4. $12 = \boxed{} - 8$

1

5. $99 + 2 = \boxed{}$

1

Marks

6.

$4 + 3 + 6 = \boxed{}$

1

7.

$36 + 7 = \boxed{}$

1

Marks

8.

20 − 6 = ⬚

1

9.

$\frac{1}{2}$ of 18 = ⬚

1

10.

$\dfrac{1}{4}$ of 20 = ⬚

1

11.

58 − 18 = ⬚

1

SCHOLASTIC Practice Papers

Marks

12.

$$25 = 19 + \boxed{}$$

1

13.

$$\boxed{} = 33 - 13$$

1

14.

$6 \times 5 = \boxed{}$

1

15.

$20 = 2 \times \boxed{}$

1

16. 36 + 27 =

Marks

1

17. 100 = ☐ + 25

1

18.

$$24 \div 2 = \boxed{}$$

1

19.

$$\frac{1}{3} \text{ of } 12 = \boxed{}$$

1

SCHOLASTIC Practice Papers

20.

$$\frac{3}{4} \text{ of } 32 = \boxed{}$$

1

21.

$$35 = \boxed{} \times 5$$

1

22.

$$43 - 30 = \boxed{}$$

1

23.

$$50 \div 10 = \boxed{}$$

1

24.

$\dfrac{2}{3}$ of 21 = ☐

Marks

1

25.

8 = ☐ ÷ 2

1

Test A: Paper 1 Marks

	Question	Possible marks	Actual marks	Workbook links
1	$7 + 3$	1		16–19
2	$10 = 8 + \boxed{}$	1		16–19
3	$69 + 1$	1		16–19
4	$12 = \boxed{} - 8$	1		16–19
5	$99 + 2$	1		16–19
6	$4 + 3 + 6$	1		16–19
7	$36 + 7$	1		16–19
8	$20 - 6$	1		16–19
9	$\frac{1}{2}$ of 18	1		33–37
10	$\frac{1}{4}$ of 20	1		33–37
11	$58 - 18$	1		16–19
12	$25 = 19 + \boxed{}$	1		16–19
13	$\boxed{} = 33 - 13$	1		16–19
14	6×5	1		23–28
15	$20 = 2 \times \boxed{}$	1		23–28
16	$36 + 27$	1		16–19
17	$100 = \boxed{} + 25$	1		16–19
18	$24 \div 2$	1		23–28
19	$\frac{1}{3}$ of 12	1		33–37
20	$\frac{3}{4}$ of 32	1		33–37
21	$35 = \boxed{} \times 5$	1		23–28
22	$43 - 30$	1		16–19
23	$50 \div 10$	1		23–28
24	$\frac{2}{3}$ of 21	1		33–37
25	$8 = \boxed{} \div 2$	1		23–28
	Total	**25**		

Mathematics

Test A: Paper 2

Instructions Test A: Paper 2

- You have around **35 minutes** to complete this test paper.
- You may **not use** a calculator for any questions in this test paper.
- Work as quickly and carefully as you can.
- Try to answer all the questions. If you cannot do one of the questions, **go on to the next one**. You can come back to it later, if you have time.
- If you finish before the end, **go back and check your work**.
- Ask your teacher if you are not sure what to do.

Follow the instructions for each question carefully.

If you need to do working out, you can use any space on the page – do not use rough paper.

Show your method

You may get extra marks if you show your method when you see this box.

> ✏ Show your method.

Aural questions

 Any questions which have this icon will be read aloud to you.

Suzie   Billy   Anaya   Ben

Practice question

1.

square

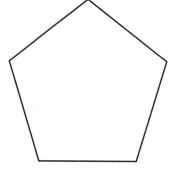

hexagon

pentagon

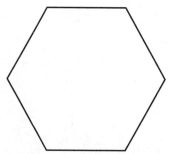

1

2.

Marks

1

3.

6   19   35   12   47

1

Marks

4.

52 [ ]

1

5.

[ ]

1

SCHOLASTIC Practice Papers

6. Fill in the missing numbers.

33, 31, ⬜ , 27 , 25 , ⬜ , 21

Marks

1

---

7. Write 48 on this number line.

←————————————————————→
40   50

Marks

1

8. Draw an arrow to show a $\frac{3}{4}$ turn in a clockwise direction.

Marks

1

9. What is the time on the clock?

Marks

1

10. Draw one line of symmetry on this shape.

1

Marks

11. Ben has 12 cherries. Anaya has twice as many cherries.

How many cherries does Anaya have?

1

---

12. Here are some signs.

| = | > | < |

Write the correct sign in each box.

25 + 3 27

8 × 2 8 + 8

1

13. Billy had 23 football stickers.

Anaya had 15.

How many more stickers did Billy have?

Marks

1

How many did they have altogether?

1

Marks

14. Mark the calculations. Use a ✓ or a ✗.

56 − 23 = 23

27 = 40 − 13

1

15. Cross out $\frac{1}{3}$ of these pennies.

Marks

1

SCHOLASTIC Practice Papers

16. What is the mass of the potatoes?

Marks

1

17. Suzie bought a bag of crisps and an apple juice.

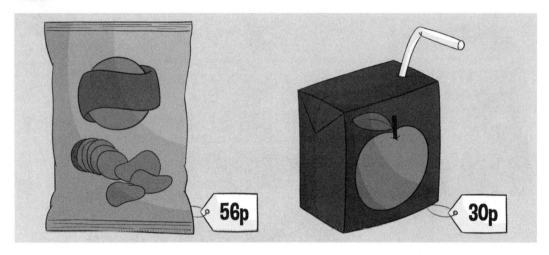

How much did Suzie spend?

Marks

1

What was her change from £1?

1

Marks

18. Complete the following calculations.

$13 + 11 =$ ☐

$11 +$ ☐ $= 24$

☐ $- 11 = 13$

$24 -$ ☐ $= 11$

2

---

19. Shade $\frac{2}{4}$ of this shape.

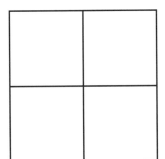

1

What fraction is equivalent to $\frac{2}{4}$?

1

20. Suzie baked 30 cookies for the school fair. She put them on plates. There were six on each plate.

How many plates did she use?

Marks

1

Ben baked half as many cookies.

How many did he bake?

1

Marks

21. The difference between 10 and 35 is 25.

Write two more **pairs** of numbers with a difference of 25.

✏ Show your method.

Pair 1 [ ] and [ ]

Pair 2 [ ] and [ ]

2

22. Billy drew this pictogram. It shows the pets that some of his friends own.

Marks

Cats	☺ ☺ ☺ ☺ ☺ ☺ ☹
Dogs	☺ ☺ ☺ ☺ ☺
Rabbits	☺ ☺ ☺ ☺
Hamsters	☺ ☺
Fish	☺ ☹

 = 2 children

How many more of his friends own cats than hamsters?

🖊 Show your method.

2

23. Complete this table.

Shape	Number of faces	Number of edges	Number of vertices
Cube			
Cuboid			
Square-based pyramid			

2

Marks

24. Billy scored 36 points on the computer game.

Anaya scored 28.

Ben scored 22.

What was the sum of their scores?

[ ]

1

How many more points than Ben did Billy score?

[ ]

1

Marks

25. Billy bought six tennis balls. Suzie bought five times as many.

Ben has half as many tennis balls as Suzie. How many does Ben have?

 Show your method.

2

Test A: Paper 2 Marks

Q	Strand	Sub-strand	Possible marks	Actual marks	Workbook links
1	Geometry	Describe properties and classify shapes	1		52–53
2	Number and place value	Read, write, order and compare numbers	1		6–13
3	Number and place value	Read, write, order and compare numbers	1		6–13
4	Number and place value	Read, write, order and compare numbers	1		6–13
5	Measurement	Money	1		46–47
6	Number and place value	Counting (in multiples)	1		6–13
7	Number and place value	Identify, represent and rounding	1		6–13
8	Geometry	Describe position, direction and movement	1		58–59
9	Measurement	Telling time, ordering time and units of time	1		49–51
10	Geometry	Describe properties and classify shapes	1		52–53
11	Calculations	Multiply/divide using written methods	1		23–32
12	Calculations	Solve problems based on all four operations	1		20–32
13	Calculations	Add/subtract to solve problems	2		16–22
14	Calculations	Add/subtract using written methods	1		16–22
15	Fractions	Recognise, find, write, name and count fractions	1		33–37
16	Measurement	Measure and read scales	1		41–42
17	Measurement	Money Solve mathematical problems involving measures	2		46–47
18	Calculations	Use inverses and check	2		18–19
19	Fractions	Recognise, find, write, name and count fractions Equivalent fractions	2		33–37
20	Calculations	Solve problems based on all four operations and knowledge of the commutative facts	2		20–32
21	Calculations	Add/subtract to solve problems	2		20–22
22	Statistics	Interpret and represent data Solve problems involving data	2		62–63
23	Geometry	Describe properties and classify shapes	2		54–55
24	Calculations	Add/subtract to solve problems	2		20–22
25	Calculations	Solve problems based on all four operations and knowledge of the commutative facts	2		20–32
		Total	**35**		

Mathematics

Test B: Paper 1

Instructions Test B: Paper 1

- You have around **20 minutes** to complete this test paper.
- You may **not use** a calculator for any questions in this test paper.
- Work as quickly and carefully as you can.
- Try to answer all the questions. If you cannot do one of the questions, **go on to the next one**. You can come back to it later, if you have time.
- If you finish before the end, **go back and check your work**.
- Ask your teacher if you are not sure what to do.

Follow the instructions for each question carefully.

If you need to do working out, you can use any space on the page – do not use rough paper.

Practice question

Marks

22 − 7 = ☐

1. [   ] $+ 4 = 10$

1

2. [   ] $= 12 + 8$

1

■SCHOLASTIC Practice Papers

Marks

3.

$14 = \boxed{} + 9$

1

4.

$34 - 10 = \boxed{}$

1

5.

$45 + 55 = \boxed{}$

1

Marks

6.

$$90 - 1 = \boxed{}$$

1

7.

$$50 = 62 - \boxed{}$$

1

SCHOLASTIC Practice Papers

Marks

8.

$5 \times \boxed{} = 50$

1

9.

$35 \div 5 = \boxed{}$

1

10.

$$74 - \boxed{} = 44$$

Marks

1

11. $46 + 38 =$

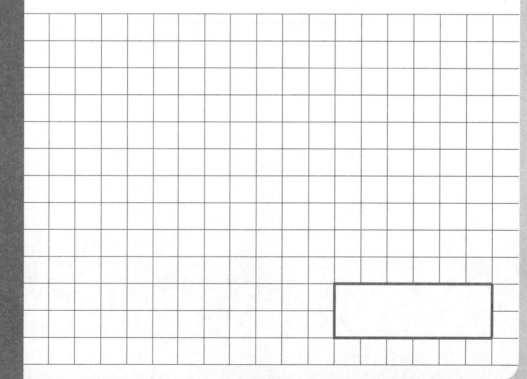

1

12.

$7 + 8 + 3 =$ [ ]

Marks

1

13.

$6 \times 3 =$ [ ]

1

Marks

14.

$$\boxed{} \times 10 = 90$$

1

15.

$$\frac{1}{2} \text{ of } 40 = \boxed{}$$

1

16.

$$\frac{3}{4} \text{ of } 12 = \boxed{}$$

Marks

1

17.

$$6 \times 2 = \boxed{} \times 6$$

1

18.

$36 - 25 = \boxed{}$

Marks

1

19.

$\dfrac{1}{2} = \dfrac{2}{\boxed{}}$

1

20.

$26 + 4 = 4 +$ ⬜

Marks

1

21.

⬜ $\div 2 = 9$

1

22.

$12 \times 10 =$ ☐

Marks

1

23.

$54 - 34 =$ ☐

1

24.

$$65 - 21 = \boxed{}$$

Marks

1

25.

$$65 + 38 =$$

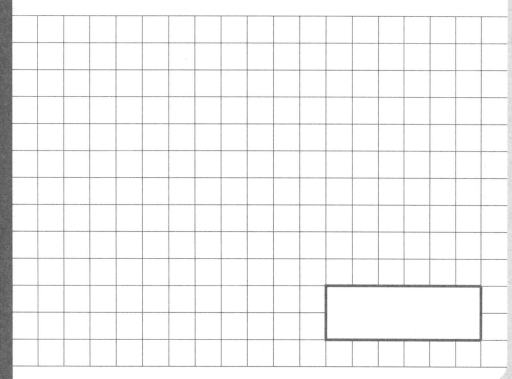

1

Test B: Paper 1 Marks

	Question	Possible marks	Actual marks	Workbook links
1	$\boxed{} + 4 = 10$	1		16–19
2	$\boxed{} = 12 + 8$	1		16–19
3	$14 = \boxed{} + 9$	1		16–19
4	$34 - 10$	1		16–19
5	$45 + 55$	1		16–19
6	$90 - 1$	1		16–19
7	$50 = 62 - \boxed{}$	1		16–19
8	$5 \times \boxed{} = 50$	1		23–28
9	$35 \div 5$	1		23–28
10	$74 - \boxed{} = 44$	1		16–19
11	$46 + 38$	1		16–19
12	$7 + 8 + 3$	1		16–19
13	6×3	1		23–28
14	$\boxed{} \times 10 = 90$	1		23–28
15	$\frac{1}{2}$ of 40	1		33–37
16	$\frac{3}{4}$ of 12	1		33–37
17	$6 \times 2 = \boxed{} \times 6$	1		23–28
18	$36 - 25$	1		16–19
19	$\frac{1}{2} = \frac{2}{\boxed{}}$	1		33–37
20	$26 + 4 = 4 + \boxed{}$	1		16–19
21	$\boxed{} \div 2 = 9$	1		23–28
22	12×10	1		23–28
23	$54 - 34$	1		16–19
24	$65 - 21$	1		16–19
25	$65 + 38$	1		16–19
Total		**25**		

Mathematics

Test B: Paper 2

Instructions Test B: Paper 2

- You have around **35 minutes** to complete this test paper.

- You may **not use** a calculator for any questions in this test paper.

- Work as quickly and carefully as you can.

- Try to answer all the questions. If you cannot do one of the questions, **go on to the next one**. You can come back to it later, if you have time.

- If you finish before the end, **go back and check your work**.

- Ask your teacher if you are not sure what to do.

Follow the instructions for each question carefully.

If you need to do working out, you can use any space on the page – do not use rough paper.

Show your method

You may get extra marks if you show your method when you see this box.

> Show your method.

Aural questions

 Any questions which have this icon will be read aloud to you.

Marks

Belle

Bruno

Annie

Harry

Test B: Paper 2

Marks

Practice question

1.

2

4   0

1

2.

7   3

[ ]   [ ]

Marks

1

3.

45   83

[ ] > [ ]

[ ] < [ ]

1

4.

Marks

triangle

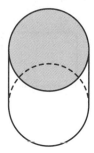

rectangle

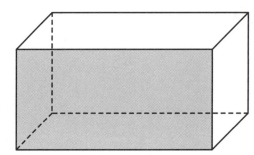

circle

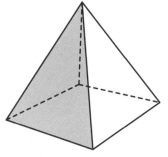

1

5.

Marks

1

---

6. Fill in the missing numbers.

2, ☐ , 3 , 3 $\frac{1}{2}$, ☐ , ☐

1

Marks

7. Harry has 24 toy cars.

Bruno has 15 toy cars.

How many more toy cars does Harry have?

1

8. Write the next **two** numbers in this sequence.

3, 6, 9, ☐ , ☐

1

Marks

9. Belle has 25 football stickers.

Harry has 45 football stickers.

How many stickers do they have altogether?

1

Marks

10. Draw a line that is 12cm long.

1

11. Use these numbers to make **two addition** and **two subtraction** statements.

15, 26, 11

1

Marks

12. Draw the next two shapes in this sequence.

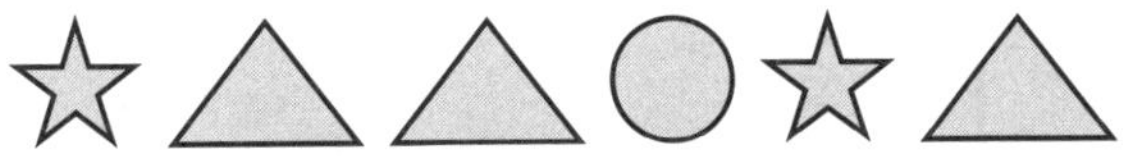

☆ △ △ ◯ ☆ △ [ ]

1

13. Annie measured a length of ribbon. It was 40cm long. She then cut it into quarters.

How long is each quarter?

[ ] cm

1

14. Look at these symbols.

| < | > | = |

Use one of them to complete the following:

100cm ☐ 1m

15. Harry has all these pencils.

Marks

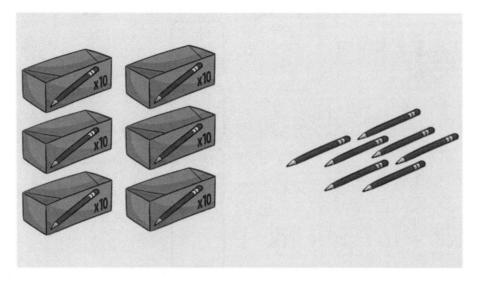

How many pencils does he have altogether?

1

He gives Belle 15 pencils.

How many does he have left?

1

16. Mark these with a ✓ or ✗.

Marks

3 × 5 = 5 × 3

12 ÷ 2 = 2 ÷ 12

7 × 5 = 5 × 7

100 ÷ 10 = 10 ÷ 100

2

Marks

17. Belle bought a notepad and pen.

59p

24p

How much did she spend altogether?

1

Marks

18. Bruno scored 80 points on the game at the arcade.

Annie scored 64.

How many more points did Bruno score than Annie?

1

How many points did they score altogether?

1

SCHOLASTIC Practice Papers

Marks

19. Count on in 3s from 21 to 33.
Write each number.

21 ☐ ☐ ☐ ☐

1

Count back in 3s from 24 to 12.
Write each number.

24 ☐ ☐ ☐ ☐

1

20. Annie shared 45 conkers equally into five pots.

How many conkers are in each pot?

1

Bruno shared 20 conkers equally into two pots.

How many conkers are in each pot?

1

Marks

21. Harry baked 30 biscuits. He put ten on a plate.

How many plates does Harry need for all his biscuits?

1

Belle also baked 30 biscuits. She put five on a plate.

How many plates does Belle need for all her biscuits?

1

22. Annie went to play with her friend.

She arrived at her friend's house at 10 minutes past 4.

She left her friend's house at 5 o'clock.

Draw the two times on these clocks

Marks

10 minutes past 4   5 o'clock

1

How long was she at her friend's house?

1

23. Bruno has 40 marbles.

Belle has twice as many marbles as Bruno.

Harry has a quarter of the number Belle has.

How many marbles does Harry have?

Marks

Show your method.

2

24. This block graph shows Class 2's favourite colours.

Marks

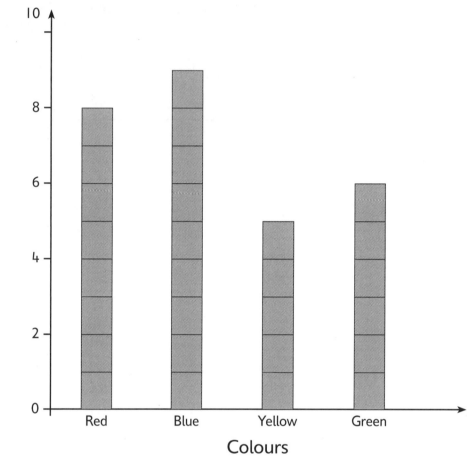

How many more children like blue than yellow?

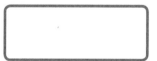

1

How many fewer children like green than red?

1

Marks

25. Annie has these coins.

Bruno has these coins.

Who has the most money?

 Show your method.

2

Test B: Paper 2 Marks

Q	Strand	Sub-strand	Possible marks	Actual marks	Workbook links
1	Number and place value	Read, write, order and compare numbers	1		6–7
2	Number and place value	Read, write, order and compare numbers	1		6–7
3	Number and place value	Read, write, order and compare numbers	1		8–10
4	Geometry	Draw and make shapes and relate 2D to 3D shapes	1		52–55
5	Measurement	Money	1		46–48
6	Fractions	Recognise, find, write, name and count fractions	1		33–37
7	Calculations	Add/subtract using written methods	1		16–22
8	Number and place value	Counting (in multiples)	1		8–9
9	Calculations	Add/subtract using written methods	1		16–22
10	Measurement	Measure and read scales	1		38–39
11	Calculations	Use inverses and check	1		18–19
12	Geometry	Patterns	1		56–57
13	Fractions	Recognise, find, write, name and count fractions	1		33–37
14	Measurement	Compare, describe and order measures	1		16–22
15	Calculations	Add/subtract to solve problems	2		16–22
16	Calculations	Solve problems based on all four operations and knowledge of the commutative facts	2		26–27
17	Measurement	Money Solve mathematical problems involving measures	1		46–48
18	Calculations	Add/subtract to solve problems	2		16–22
19	Number and place value	Counting (in multiples)	2		8–9
20	Calculations	Solve problems based on all four operations and knowledge of the commutative facts	2		29–32
21	Calculations	Solve problems based on all four operations and knowledge of the commutative facts	2		29–32
22	Measurement	Telling time, ordering time and units of time	2		49–51
23	Calculations	Solve problems based on all four operations and knowledge of the commutative facts	2		29–32
24	Statistics	Interpret and represent data	2		62–63
25	Measurement	Money	2		46–48
		Total	**35**		

Marks & guidance

Marking and assessing the papers

The mark schemes and answers are located towards the end of this booklet.

The mark schemes provide details of correct answers including guidance for questions that have more than one mark.

Interpreting answers

Problem	Guidance
Digit has been written in reverse.	A reversed digit is acceptable if it is clearly recognisable as the digit intended. For example, a reversed 2 must clearly show the characteristics of a 2 rather than a 5.
The number has been transposed in the answer.	Transposed numbers should not be awarded the mark. For example, an answer of '16' when the correct answer is '61' should not be marked as correct.
The answer is equivalent to the one in the mark scheme.	The mark scheme will generally specify which equivalent responses are allowed. If this is not the case, award the mark unless the mark scheme states otherwise. For example: $1\frac{1}{2}$ or 1.5.
The answer is correct but the wrong working is shown.	Always award the mark(s) for a correct response unless the mark scheme states otherwise.
The correct response has been crossed (or rubbed) out and not replaced.	Do not award the mark(s) for legible crossed-out answers that have not been replaced or that have been replaced by a further incorrect attempt.
The answer has been worked out correctly but an incorrect answer has been written in the answer box.	Give precedence to the answer given in the answer box over any other workings. There may be cases where the incorrect answer is due to a transcription error. You may check the child's intention and decide whether to award the mark.
More than one answer is given.	If all answers given are correct (or a range of answers is given, all of which are correct), award the mark unless the mark scheme states otherwise. If both correct and incorrect responses are given, do not award the mark unless the mark scheme states otherwise.

Problem	Guidance
There appears to be a misread of numbers affecting the working.	In general, the mark should not be awarded. However, in two-mark questions that have a working mark, award one mark if the working is applied correctly using the misread numbers, provided that the misread numbers are comparable in difficulty to the original numbers. For example, if '243' is misread as '234', both numbers may be regarded as comparable in difficulty.
No answer is given in the expected place, but the correct answer is given elsewhere.	Where a child has shown understanding of the question, award the mark. In particular, where a word or number response is expected, a child may meet the requirement by annotating a graph or labelling a diagram elsewhere in the question.

Written methods for addition and subtraction

The following guidance shows some written methods suitable for Key Stage 1.

Addition

$$25 + 34 = 20 + 5 + 30 + 4$$
$$= 20 + 30 + 5 + 4$$
$$= 50 + 9$$
$$= 59$$

```
   2  5  =  2  0  +  5
+  3  4  =  3  0  +  4
   ‾‾‾‾‾     ‾‾‾‾‾‾‾‾‾‾
   5  9     5  0  +  9
```

Subtraction

$$54 - 33$$

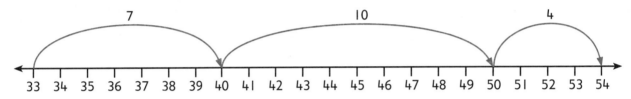

$$54 - 33 = 7 + 10 + 4 = 21$$

```
   5  4  =  5  0  +  4
-  3  3  =  3  0  +  3
   ‾‾‾‾‾     ‾‾‾‾‾‾‾‾‾‾
   2  1     2  0  +  1
```

National standard in maths

The mark that your child gets in the test paper will be known as the 'raw score' (for example, '28' in 28/60). The raw score will be converted to a scaled score and children achieving a scaled scored of 100 or more will achieve the National Standard in that subject. The DfE will be introducing a conversion table to create a 'scaled score' for the tests. A 'scaled score' will enable results to be reported consistently year-on-year.

The guidance in the table below shows the marks that children need to achieve to reach the National Standard. This should be treated as a guide only as the number of marks may vary. You can also find up-to-date information about scaled scores on our website: www.scholastic.co.uk/nationaltests

Total mark achieved	Standard
0–33	Has not met the national standard in mathematics for Year 2
34–60	Has met the national standard in mathematics for Year 2

Aural questions

Explain to the children that you will read aloud some questions for them to answer. Tell them that you will read each question twice only, leaving a short gap in-between. Tell the children that they must listen very carefully when you read the questions.

Do the practice question together. Check that the children have written the answer in the box.

Read aloud questions 1 to 5 and repeat the question (the bold text only). Tell the children that they must work on their own and they must not call out the answers.

Remember to repeat the question. Repeat the bold text only. At the end of each question, allow sufficient time for the children to complete what they can.

TEST A, PAPER 2 (pages 12-14)

Practice question: **What is 15 subtract 10?** Write your answer in the box.

1. **Draw a line from the shape to its name.**

2. **Suzie thought of a number. It had 9 ones and 5 tens.** Write the number in the box.

3. **Circle the odd numbers.**

4. **Write 52 in words.**

5. **Ben has these coins in his pocket. How much money does he have?**

TEST B, PAPER 2 (pages 68-71)

Practice question: **What is 12 multiplied by 10?** Write your answer in the box.

1. **What number can be made using these cards?**

2. **What two numbers can be made using both the digits 7 and 3?**

3. **Write two number sentences to compare 45 and 83.** Use the greater than and less than symbols.

4. **What 2D shapes can you see on the 3D shapes?** Draw a line from the name to the shape.

5. **How much money can you see?**

Mark scheme Test A: Paper 1 (pages 9-23)

Q	Answers	Marks
Practice	7	
1	10	1
2	2	1
3	70	1
4	20	1
5	101	1
6	13	1
7	43	1
8	14	1
9	9	1
10	5	1
11	40	1
12	6	1
13	20	1
14	30	1
15	10	1
16	63	1
17	75	1
18	12	1
19	4	1
20	24	1
21	7	1
22	13	1
23	5	1
24	14	1
25	16	1
	Total	**25**

Mark scheme Test A: Paper 2 (pages 25-47)

Q	Answers	Marks
Practice	5	
I	 **Award I mark** only if all answers are correct.	I
2	59	I
3	Circled numbers are: 19, 35, 47 **Award I mark** only if all answers are correct.	I
4	Fifty-two Allow misspellings if intention is clear.	I
5	42(p)	I
6	29, 23 Award I mark only if all answers are correct.	I
7		I
8		I
9	Accept 45 minutes past 7, 15 minutes to 8, $\frac{1}{4}$ to 8, quarter to eight, 7:45.	I
10	 Accept slight inaccuracies in the line of symmetry as long as the intention is clear. (As a guide, the line of symmetry should be within 3mm of a vertex, or the midpoint of the shape.)	I
II	24	I

Q	Answers	Marks
12	$25 + 3 > 27$ $8 \times 2 = 8 + 8$ **Award 1 mark** only if both answers are correct.	1
13	8 38	1 1
14	$56 - 23 = 23$ ✗ $27 = 40 - 13$ ✓ **Award 1 mark** only if both answers are correct.	1
15	**Award 1 mark** for 7 pennies crossed out.	1
16	$2\frac{1}{2}$(kg) or 2.5(kg)	1
17	86(p) 14(p)	1 1
18	$13 + 11 = \mathbf{24}$ $11 + \mathbf{13} = 24$ $\mathbf{24} - 11 = 13$ $24 - \mathbf{13} = 11$ **Award 1 mark** if two or three answers are correct. **Award 2 marks** if all answers are correct.	2
19	Accept any shading of two quarters. $\frac{1}{2}$ or any other equivalent fraction	1 1
20	5 15	1 1
21	Any pairs of numbers with a difference of 25 **Award 1 mark** if one correct pair is given. **Award 2 marks** if two correct pairs are given.	2
22	9 **Award 1 mark** if the numbers 13 and 4 have been indicated but the subtraction is incorrect. **Award 2 marks** for a correct response of 9.	2

Q	Answers	Marks
23		2

Shape	Number of faces	Number of edges	Number of vertices
Cube	6	12	8
Cuboid	6	12	8
Square-based pyramid	5	8	5

Award 1 mark if the answers for two shapes are correct.
Award 2 marks if the answers for three shapes are correct.

Q	Answers	Marks
24	86	1
	14	1
25	15	2
	Award 1 mark if 30 is given when working out.	
	Award 2 marks for the correct answer.	
	Total	**35**

SCHOLASTIC Guidance and mark schemes

Q	Answers	Marks
Practice	15	
1	6	1
2	20	1
3	5	1
4	24	1
5	100	1
6	89	1
7	12	1
8	10	1
9	7	1
10	30	1
11	84	1
12	18	1
13	18	1
14	9	1
15	20	1
16	9	1
17	2	1
18	11	1
19	4	1
20	26	1
21	18	1
22	120	1
23	20	1
24	44	1
25	103	1
	Total	25

Q	Answers	Marks
Practice	120	
1	42	1
2	37, 73 **Award 1 mark** only if both answers are correct.	1
3	83 > 45, 45 < 83 **Award 1 mark** only if both answers are correct.	1
4	 triangle — rectangle — circle matched to shapes **Award 1 mark** only if all answers are correct.	1
5	£1.63	1
6	$2\frac{1}{2}, 4, 4\frac{1}{2}$ **Award 1 mark** only if all answers are correct.	1
7	9 toy cars	1
8	12, 15 **Award 1 mark** only if both answers are correct.	1
9	70	1
10	Line must be exactly 12cm in length	1
11	15 + 11 = 26 11 + 15 = 26 26 − 15 = 11 26 − 11 = 13 **Award 1 mark** only if all answers are correct.	1
12	Drawing of a triangle followed by a circle	1

SCHOLASTIC Guidance and mark schemes

Q	Answers	Marks
13	10(cm)	1
14	100 cm = 1m	1
15	67	1
	52	1
16	3 × 5 = 5 × 3 ✓ 12 ÷ 2 = 2 ÷ 12 ✗ 7 × 5 = 5 × 7 ✓ 100 ÷ 10 = 10 ÷ 100 ✗ **Award 1 mark** if 3 answers are correct. **Award 2 marks** if all answers are correct.	2
17	83p	1
18	16	1
	144	1
19	24, 27, 30, 33	1
	21, 18, 15, 12	1
20	9	1
	10	1
21	3	1
	6	1
22	Hands correctly positioned to show 10 past 4 and 5 o'clock	1
	50 minutes	1
23	20 **Award 2 marks** if correct answer obtained. **Award 1 mark** if part of the answer is correct. For example, Belle has 80 marbles.	2
24	4	1
	2	1
25	Annie **Award 2 marks** if correct answer obtained, with workings shown. **Award 1 mark** if answer incorrect but method shows evidence of understanding of the process required. For example, Annie's money has been correctly totalled to 78p or Bruno's to 75p.	2
	Total	**35**

Notes

Notes

SCHOLASTIC

NATIONAL CURRICULUM
MATHS
BOOSTER TESTS
YEAR 2

BOOSTER TESTS

Set A

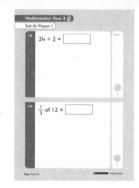

Paper 1
Arithmetic

Paper 2
Reasoning

✔ **Get children used to the SATs format**

Give your children a boost with the most authentic practice papers for the National Tests

Set B

✔ **All the support you need!**

Each test comes with a full mark scheme and clear guidance so you can check progress

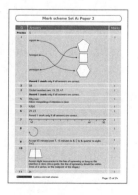

✔ **Great value for money!**

In this book, you get two complete tests, plus detailed answers and guidance

Paper 1
Arithmetic

Paper 2
Reasoning

Keep on track with other key Scholastic titles:

National Curriculum Maths Practice Book Year 2
ISBN 978-1407-12889-4

SATs Made Simple: Year 2 Maths
ISBN 978-1407-18327-5

Guidance and mark schemes

Maths Booster
Tests for Year 2

£7.99

SCHOLASTIC

ISBN 978-1-407-18360-2

9 781407 183602

www.scholastic.co.uk